THE MAN WHO WON WITHOUT FIGHTING

JUDGES 6 and 7 FOR CHILDREN

Written by Yvonne Holloway McCall

Illustrated by Vaccaro Associates

Concordia Publishing House

ARCH Books

Copyright © 1971 Concordia Publishing House, St. Louis, Missouri
Concordia Publishing House Ltd., London, E. C. 1
Manufactured in the United States of America
All Rights Reserved
ISBN 0-570-06060-5

Gideon hid his bundles of wheat,
for spies were out scouting for something to eat.
He crouched in the shadows and watched till at last
the thieves and their camels had traveled past.

Then he jumped, for behind him someone spoke —
an angel who sat in the shade of an oak.
And he said, "What a mighty leader you'll be!
You'll set all the people of Israel free."
"Rescue us all from the people of Midian?
Who, me? But how could that be?" cried Gideon.

Then he prayed, "Dear God, if it's really so,
please use this sheepskin to let me know.
If You want me to gather my men in a band
and drive the enemy out of the land,
let the fleece be soaking and wet as winter,
the ground be dusty and dry as a splinter."

Next morning, before the sun was high,
the fleece was wet, and the ground was dry.

But Gideon said, "To be *sure* that I'm right,
I'll put out the fleece again tonight.
Let the fleece be dry and fluffy, and yet
let the ground all around be soggy and wet."

In the morning the ground was damp with dew, but the fleece was dry, as good as new.

So he gathered an army of men on the hill,
and they stooped by a river to drink their fill.
Some cupped their hands to their mouths to drink,
some knelt with their mouths in the watery brink.

Then God said, "The ones
with their mouths in the foam,
that kneel at the edge of the water, send home."
So Gideon sent away rank after rank
till only a handful were left on the bank.

Then Gideon frowned as he saw the foe –
the enemy camped in the valley below,
covering the country for miles all around
like thousands of grasshoppers
clumped on the ground.
And Gideon's frown grew deeper still
as he counted his three hundred men on the hill.

"If you'll do as I say," God told him, "you'll win
though your army is small
and your ranks are thin."
And continuing then, He explained to Gideon
how to defeat the army of Midian.

So Gideon commanded,
"Split up in three groups.
In the night they will think
we have many more troops.
I'm handing each man a trumpet to blow.
When the time is right, I'll let you know.

Then shout at the enemy troops of Midian,
'The sword of the Lord and the sword of Gideon.'
Now light your torches,
but keep them from showing;
put them in jugs to hide their glowing."

So with torches in jugs to hide the light,
they followed their leader late in the night.

As they quietly crept down the steep, dark hill,
the enemy camp lay sleeping and still.

At the signal they shouted as trumpets blew,
"The sword of the Lord and of Gideon too."
They smashed their jugs, and the torches spread
into flaring flames of orange and red.

The smashing noise, the torchlight glare,
the trumpets at night with scary blare
jolted each enemy soldier awake,
and in all the confusion they made a mistake.

They fought one another, and then in dread,
helter-skelter they turned and fled.

So God's clever plan of trumpets and lighting
made Gideon win without any fighting.
His people were safe. They shouted and roared
for Gideon, their leader, who followed the Lord,
"You conquered our foes. You're ever so clever.
You saved us. Now rule us as king forever."
"No," replied Gideon, "for though it seems odd,
I'm not the hero. The hero is God."

DEAR PARENTS:

The story of Gideon is the story of God's merciful and surprising deliverance. The people of Israel cried for help to the Lord because they were "brought very low because of Midian."

The usual way to overpower an enemy is to assemble a large army and build up superior strength. Perhaps the people prayed for military might to throw off the oppression of the Midianites.

But God had His own plan to show mercy to His people. Instead of choosing the most popular man or the mightiest military leader, He selected an unknown farmer named Gideon to be the leader of His people. Gideon could hardly believe that God would choose such a humble man as he, but God convinced him.

Gideon believed in the Lord. He had faith that God would use him, a humble man, and very humble means and methods to overcome the Midianites. Three hundred men with trumpets, torches, and earthen jars were enough. Gideon won the battle without fighting, but he knew it was God who really won the battle.

This story strengthens our faith in our faithful God. He often used ordinary things to achieve His purpose. He once came as a helpless child, born of a humble mother, and lived a poor life among men to redeem us from evil.

THE EDITOR